To whoever fi...

I hope you find
your power.
xoxo - Leah

tik tok: elleunchained

Truth Bombs for Fuckboys

Also by the author in this series…

Truth Bombs For Fuckboys

Poems about Anger

Leah Cass

Soul Revitalization LLC

Copyright © 2022 Leah Cass

ISBN: 978-1-960143-01-3

DEDICATION

This book is dedicated to the loves our lives, who force us to grow.

TABLE OF CONTENTS

Preface

This book isn't about him. This book isn't about her. This book is about you for once. This book is about claiming your power, seeing through the bullshit, and walking in a direction that serves you better. This book isn't a letter of hate to those who have hurt us. This book is a love letter to ourselves.

This is your permission slip to be powerful.

I'm not a perfect feminist. I am not a fully actualized person. This book isn't a shining example of the perfect ways to deal with heartbreak; but it's real and it's raw and it's true.

But make no mistake: my intention is not to glorify these emotions. It is to write them down and then light them on fire and set them free. I don't want to carry them anymore.

Life is too short to focus on anything less than full liberation.

Trigger

You might have been vain
But this song was always
About you

Irony

I drink these spirits
to keep your spirit
out

each shot
burning sage
blurring my vision

burning
your image
away

12 Steps

When we traded hearts
So much of yours was missing
And so heavy was
The whole of mine

But It's Still Beating

I wanted to hear the sound of
Your heart pulsating inside
The caverns of your chest

Mine is still stretched
And bruised and silent
From letting you back in

Prodigal Sun

How fragile were
These heartstrings
On which you played

Strumming

This probably works

For your pool of fives
With low self esteem
But baby-
There are different rules
When you are batting
out of your league

Maybe I am Kind of a Bitch

Shrouded by delusions of grandeur
Lonely little boys flee
When exposed
To the safety of their
Own rationalizations

Tale as Old as Time

Tossed away
Always the collateral damage of
A coward's game

Does This Make Me Property?

But I'll grow tired
Of waiting when you're finally ready
And you'll be the one who cries

Comeuppance

I've been to the bottom
Of the shallow recesses of your soul
And seen all there is to see
If this is all you have to offer
Bring the check please

Going Dutch

Leaving was your greatest talent
And missing you was mine
We made a perfect team

Teamwork Makes the Dream Work

I languished in solitude
Listening to the pitter patter
Of rain drops and the wind
Whispering your name
But the sun was shining
In a different place

Tropic of Cancer

Escalation

I still wonder if
You count me on
Your fingers when
You think of all
The girls you've loved

There Was Ten in the Bed and the Little One Said
Roll Over

We bleed the same blood,
You and me, but
I pick at my own scabs repeatedly
Creating bigger scars and uglier
Skin, slowed healing
While you tie your Band-Aid
Wound with a tourniquet
So tight you're losing limbs
Disregarding the day
You ever try to walk again

Physical Therapy

Once
We felt alive
Propeller roaring
Behind us
Water so clear
We could see through
To the bottom's slimy rocks
Coolers full of Miller Lites
That seemed so refreshing
Before my palate changed

Once

But even your honesty
Was full of lies
I dare you to be
Honest one more time

Truth or Dare

I'll write his fantasies
Long after his realities
Have been forgotten
The immortal muse
Of my imagination
Possibilities only rendered
In my creation

If a Writer Loves You, Your Sins Will Never Die

I'm not good with words I just
Drip the highs and lows of
Dopamine and serotonin
Into your veins through
IV's of paper

While the demons
Whistle by in the dark

Escaping

So I shut the door
And drove a thousand miles
Your face in my rearview mirror
Larger than you will ever appear

Florida

Change rustles in our wind
Taking me freely
And even you, in your rigidity
Hard gusts transplanting
Our molecules to some
Unknown place

All I wanted was to dream with you
But alone instead I lay awake
Drying my tears on your pillow
To drown in your scent
And you dream of me now
While you listen to Drake

But if You're Reading This
It's Too Damn Late

How the tables
have turned
I'll take my
peanut butter fudge
gelato while you
feast on your
fifty shades of
store brand, generic
Vanilla

Premium

I inhaled
your poison
to treat my disease
My suicide began
with you

Assisted

I can heal myself
I can love myself
I can feed myself
I can fuck myself
ALL I wanted
From you
Was conversation

Remembering Who the Fuck I am

Men

Help conceive you then
blame you for existing
grab your hand at parties
and move it to their dick quietly
knowing you don't want a scene

imply things they will never say to make you theirs
without being yours
eat the cake of your presence
while having their freedom too
put you on a pedestal so high
you can't talk over the wind
but no one was listening anyways

Men

Fuck your mind as much as your body
Call you crazy if you figure it out
cowards repeating
you don't know what you're
doing to me with those green eyes
girl

Detritus

I've learned to
squeeze myself into
the corners of my mind
where you never existed

But sometimes
you still knock
at the door
in the middle
of the night

Intruder

I wanted you then
When I still
Believed in
Lies and love
As if there were a difference

Meditation

Maybe I am a god
I created you
in my image
more perfect and original

Maybe I am a god
I loved you
from a distance
and you shunned me too

Blasphemy

Sometimes bridges
aren't burned
they are washed away
by the flood of
too many cries
too many times
too many tries

Crying and Listening to Selena Gomez

Sometimes
on good days I dream
that there could still be
A shred of hope

But I've never suffered
fools kindly

and a fool you were to let me go

Lose you to love me

You never really knew me
If you thought I would lose
Myself to win your games
I could always see right through you
But
I would have loved you anyways

The Heart Wants What It Wants

Crisis

Sometimes
I still stroke the
silky strands
that remain
between us
only the devil still
connects me to you

Thanatophobia

I thought
I escaped

but in a
split second
of weakness

here you are
slowly killing me
again

and I somehow relish the taste

Cigarettes in the Morning

I still miss
your toxicity
complicity
the way you
burned right
through the
inside of me

The Body Keeps the Score

My faith has
Finally been restored
but in myself alone
nothing more

Clarity

I loved the way
you bent my thoughts
the way you made me bleed
the way you broke through all my rusty locks
I loved your flowers and your weeds

Secret Gardens

When I die
bury me in the weight
of your empty promises
how I love to
carry them in life

Strapped

Once upon a time
I believed in your magic
And I would watch with glee
As you pulled rabbits
Out of your hat
But it was all timed, faked, planted
And I can't settle for tricks when I am the real thing

I Hear the Jury is Still out on Science

I've made you
immortal with
the ink of my tears

I gave you your life
I can take it away

Emptying Pens and Notebooks

Free
from the tyranny
Of you and me
I breathe
Waiting to feel
Whole again

In the Autumn Sunshine

I lost you once
In the eruption of
Time's illusion and
Our cells dividing

Once the smoke cleared
You still were there
Caked in dried blood
And silence

Mount Vesuvius

I won't
Bow down
In solemn
Compliance

I won't
Pretend
To be
Sane

Institutionalized

I must have loved you
A thousand times
For I carry the grief
Of a thousand lives

Layers in the Shadows

I grew and grew
away from you
until my head was
in the stars
staring down
at the speck of your darkness.

I, Alone, Proceed

I won that day
You chose your games
Over the simple truth

And now every time I come
I come a little harder
Knowing it will never be with you

Living Well is the Best Revenge

I romanced your demons
long after you'd forsaken mine
but they made such good conversation
I never noticed you'd gone

Incubus

Recovery

I am not ashamed
Of how deeply I feel
I might have been crazy
But at least

I Was Real

If you thought
I was the kind of girl
Who would wait for you
Cave for you
Play for you
I'm not the one
Who is crazy

Truth Bombs for Fuckboys

I wrote an ode
To yesterday's
Dust and the
Particles of you
That landed beside me

And the flowers
That grew in the
Place where you lay
Somewhere right behind me

Carbon

Some men love the idea of you
They'll day dream about running
Their hands through your bangs
While you teach them how to smile
Again but when you are a real
Person they will leave

At Least We Tried

Maybe you hate that
in spite of myself
I can always tell
exactly what you're thinking
I pray to god to make it stop
but he has left me out here sinking

Earmuffs

I still worship you
in secret
with these hymns
with this hate

Take Me to Church

I planted my seeds
in your scorched earth
how foolish to think they might grow

Battlefields

I washed you
out of my hair today
the suds slipped down my back
swirled down the drain

South Pacific

How long did you think
You could hold my power?
I was only loaning,
Always taking it back.

Understudy

Maybe I imagined
that if I ripped off my scabs
and bled for you
it would heal
your wounds
and maybe,
just maybe
you would
love me too

Pathetic

All the footsteps between us
have disintegrated, erased
by the elements and the passage
of time and new people
walking on top
Maybe they never existed

I dreamt once they were fresh
again, and new and they led me
to you and you had changed
but not enough

And That's When I Carried Me

You hang
on every word
I speak
in silence
but I see
you in the
corner, dark
still and quiet

I can feel your heart
beating, its tumult, its violence

Muted

The worst part
isn't even knowing
I was used
it's remembering
how willfully
and patiently
I took the abuse

Self Loathing

If only
You had twisted
Me in your sheets
The way i
Twisted in
Your mind

There's No Sex in Your Violence

You took a picture of me
cut it out of cardboard
propped it up and
loved it instead
I looked so fucking pretty

Mirage

When I am gone
will you mourn
my destruction or
simply observe it
from afar with
detached interest
the way you did it in life?

Sit by My Tomb and Tell Me a Story

Depression

In you I imagined
A depth that never
Existed
It was glimpses of myself
I found
A fire dormant
Far too long

But Sparks were Ignited

Hope
My only drug
Self medication
Still low
From the high
Shaky withdrawal
Slowly weaning
My addiction

Absinthe

And we stumble again
You and i
As the four horsemen
Of the apocalypse
Come galloping by

Blast the Trumpets

Sometimes there was magic
Sometimes we could roll out a blanket under
The starry sky
kiss and pretend
There was more than lust and loneliness and fear

Sometimes there was magic
We could drive to West Virginia at midnight
Reeking of youth and indifference
Pretending it wasn't a rum soaked fantasy

Sometimes there was magic
We could believe cigarettes will never
Kill us
and that we weren't already dead
You always knew how to comfort me when I cried

Sometimes there was magic

We drove all night

without destination
gas paid with crumpled one dollar bills
soaked in grease and sweat
from the diner behind us
reality eclipsed by
vague dreams and pure hearts still unbroken
drunk off Zima and
rescued from our demons
by boys we barely knew
who uttered I love you
far too quickly
Colorblind
to red flags
our love
their power
corrupted absolutely

I Write Sins, Not Tragedies

For what kind of life
can you truly live
when your thoughts
are marred with
taunting what ifs

Help me up
I've fallen
Into the bottom
Of my own insanity

And somehow now
I want to live
To see the other side

Present

I guess I knew
Deep down
That you would
Fail the test

Every time
We meet as strangers
I love you just
A little less

Catfished

I've started to
like myself more
since I've let my
clothes fall smooth
from my skin to the floor

Authenticity

She was born of fire
but never tasted the ash

I walked on her coals
I grinned through the pain

Propelled by desire
immune to the flames
I'd found reclamation at last

Phoenix

I am not a black hole where
The sun goes to die
I am sun
I am wind
I am rain
I am sky

Goddess Shit

I do not write---
My tears just fall
on the paper
arranged
in words.

Their Fire Burns

I only miss you when
the silence fills with
the echoes of your voice
reverberating through my insides
when I embraced the hiraeth
and let the specters of yearning dance
between twisted bodies
almost combined but now forgotten
Possibilities lost, buried
Deep in recesses of the past

Hiraeth

Every time she shattered
she picked up the pretty little pieces
and built a new mosaic
hands scarred
from the jagged
colored glass

Mosaic

I loved you once
drunk on lazy, foolish youth

before the wanderlust creeped
into my unarmed heart
sweeping me from
you, the only home I ever had

Now I sit trapped
in the echoes of
the ghosts of Christmas past
dust covered photo albums

with smiling faces
preserved for a future that
never was
or will be

I needed you once
drunk on lazy, foolish youth

1 Corinthians 13:11

Be still my nomad heart
At the sight of
The open road

Hearts skip beating
At the view ahead
Finally free

I drive
Wind whipping through my hair
Wild
As the fresh air clears
Out the mildewy smell
Of yesterday's sorrows

I Whip My Hair Back and Forth

Even on the darkest days
Sunshine awaits
Behind the thick clouds
Peeking through only
After precipitation's release

Hope

But baby I burned for you
like it was some kind of fucking virtue

I would say sorry for going crazy
but we both know it will happen again

Facts

ACKNOWLEDGMENTS

I would not be anywhere without my family. Thank you to Bill, Kaylee, Eliza, Vanessa, William, Jason, and Lois. Huge thank you to Aimee, who helped me edit and format and calmed me down when I needed it. Special shout out to Instagram as well, and all the followers who believed in me when I was just sad and trying to feel better. Thank you to my soul family, for believing in me and always encouraging me. And thank you to my dad. I wish you were still here to see it.

End Notes

1. This series is an homage to the five stages of grief model was developed by **Elisabeth Kübler-Ross**, and became famous after she published her book On Death and Dying in 1969.

2. Chapters are based on the five stages of anger, according to the Anger Arousal Model commonly used in anger management classes.

3. Page 5- Carly Simon reference

4. Page 6 – Alcoholics Anonymous reference

5. Page 26 – Drake reference

6. Pages 34-36 are all Selena Gomez references (should I dedicate this book to her?)

7. Page 39- Thanatophobia is fear of death.

8. Page 41- The Body Keeps the Score by Bessel Van Der Kolk, 2015

9. Page 45- reference to "Walk Hard: The Dewey Cox Story" - 2007 by Columbia Pictures

10. Page 62- Hosier

11. Page 64 - South Pacific

12. Page 67- that poem about footsteps and Jesus carrying you

13. Page 70- Bush

14. Page 79 - the classic Panic at the Disco song

15. Page 86- Hiraeth is the longing for a home that never existed

16. Page 88- *1 Corinthians 13:11: "When I was a child, I talked like a child, I thought like a child, I reasoned like a child. When I became a man, I put the ways of childhood behind me." New International Version*

17. Page 89- reference to Willow Smith

ABOUT THE AUTHOR

Leah Cass is a poet, writer, mental health advocate, and lover of all things spiritual. She currently resides in Pittsburgh, PA with her husband, daughter, and two spoiled cats. She graduated from Chatham University with a bachelor's degree in Psychology and continued her education in clinical mental health counseling at Duquesne University.

A strong believer in the power of story to build community and spark healing, Leah loves using her voice to help others open up about their own experiences with mental health and personal growth. She frequently speaks at events and workshops on topics such as mental health awareness, post traumatic growth, and self-care. You can find her on Instagram as @elleunchained.

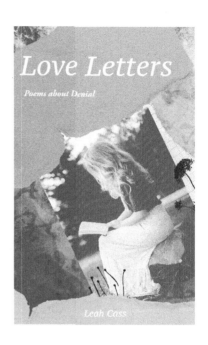